Buried Treasure

15 drama sketches for church and school

Tony Bower

Kevin
Mayhew

First published in 1998
This edition published in 2001 by
KEVIN MAYHEW LTD
Buxhall
Stowmarket
Suffolk 1P14 3BW

0 1 2 3 4 5 6 7 8 9

ISBN 1 84003 702 4
Catalogue Number 1500412

Cover design by Jonathan Stroulger, cartoon by Jonathan Whalley
Edited and typeset by Elisabeth Bates

Printed in Great Britain

Contents

About the author

Tony Bower is a full-time schools worker with Northern Inter-Schools Christian Union.

He is experienced in writing and performing drama in a variety of contexts including schools, youth groups and churches.

He likes playing football, walking, reading, writing and drinking coffee but not all at the same time!

Tony is married to Claire and they have a son, Joseph.

'I'm a lifelong Barnsley fan, a sentence I was given at birth. I feel better for confessing that fact. I feel even better now that you have bought this book. I would feel absolutely ecstatic if you performed these sketches to share the good news of the gospel of Jesus Christ.'

Drama techniques

Maybe you have been acting since the moment you first began to walk, or maybe this is your first time of treading the boards. The sketches in this book are written specifically as short, attention grabbing, audience holding, easy learning for two people talking. Therefore they should not take too much time to learn.

'HOORAY!' I hear you cry!

However, basic drama techniques need to be adhered to for the best effect. So whether you are an absolute beginner or an academy award winner, here are a few pointers and guidelines to help you along the way.

A lot of techniques are basic and simple – for example, projection.

Things to consider in making a sketch interesting

- Movement
- Levels
- Character
- Interaction
- Surprise
- Mystery
- Humorous
- Attention-grabbing

Four simple steps to performing a sketch

1. Get a script – one that says what you want to communicate.
2. Learn the lines – saves rehearsal time.
3. Rehearse – make sure that everyone is confident.
4. Ask someone to 'direct' or watch – other people may see basic things you might otherwise miss.

In these sketches, where the male gender is used the female gender may be substituted, and vice versa, where appropriate, at the discretion of the producer.

Buried treasure

The message

To look at what people are living for.
What do they value the most? What is their treasure?

Characters

1 = treasure seeker
2 = newspaper reader

Setting the scene

A person digging frantically. They pause to wipe their brow.

Script

1   It's got to be here. It has to be here. *(Begins digging again)* I must find it, I must. *(Stops digging, puts the spade down and starts to dig with his hands. A man walks onto stage, busy reading a newspaper which he holds in front of his face. Unaware of the man lying down on the ground he trips over him.)* Ouch!

2   Oops.

1   What do you think you are doing?

2   What do you think you are doing?

     (1 stands up, looks around very anxiously, head darting in all directions. Leans towards the other person then speaks in a whisper.)

1   It's a secret.

2   What's a secret?

1   I can't say. It's a secret.

2   Wait a minute. You can't go around digging a hole in the park.

1   Why not?

2   It's council property.

1   Oh.

2   You've not thought of that, have you?

1   No.

2   So you'd better stop, fill in the hole, go home and get a wash.

1   But I can't.

2   Yes, you can. Pick up your spade and fill the hole.

1   No, I can't.

2   Why not?

1   Not until . . .

2   *(Starting to get exasperated)* Not until what?

1   It's a secret.

2   Look, if you don't tell me what you are up to I'm going to report you to the park keeper.

1   Secrets are secrets, I won't tell, I won't, I won't. *(Folds arms and pouts)*

2   If that's your attitude you leave me no choice. *(2 begins to walk off. 1 runs to stop 2. 1 stands in front of 2 blocking his way. 2 tries to move to one side and then is blocked, moves to the other side and is blocked again.)*

1   You can't go to the park keeper. You can't tell anyone.

2   Yes, I can.

1   No, you can't.

2   Yes, I can.

1   No, you can't.

2   Yes, I can.

1   No, you can't.

2   Yes, I can. *(Pushes past and strides away)*

1   OK, I'll tell. *(2 stops)* Promise you'll keep a secret.

2   Why?

1   Please, promise.

2   Maybe . . . just tell me.

(1 looks around again. Points to the ground, speaking in a hushed voice.)

1   Treasure.

2   Treasure?

1   Gold.

2   Gold!

1   Shh!

2   There's no treasure in this park.

1   Look at this. *(1 pulls out a map from a pocket)*

2   Where did you get it from? *(1 gives 2 a stare)* Don't tell me it's a secret.

1   Yes.

2   You weren't given this on April 1st, were you?

1   How did you know?

2   April Fool's Day? Treasure maps? 200-year-old treasure buried in a park 22 years old?

1   No, it can't be. You mean this is a practical joke?

2   I am afraid so. Good job you found out before you dug all the park up.

1   I wish you had told me earlier.

(2 walks away and falls into a hole)

1   Mind those holes.

Application

How silly to dig up the ground looking for gold. What realistic chance was there of finding any? Yet people pay money each week trying to win the lottery. More fool's gold. We have been sold a lie, that riches bring happiness and fulfilment in life. They don't. So what does?
Go on to talk about real lasting treasure.

Discussion starters

• What do people treasure in life?
• Why are we looking for something of real worth?
• What kind of treasure can last?

Bible verses

• Matthew 6:19-20
• 1 Peter 1:3-7

Guilty

The message

To look at the fact that people do not always look at the evidence about God. Sometimes people have their own preconceived ideas, their minds are already made up.

Characters

1 = foreman
2 = judge

Setting the scene

A courtroom. There is a judge sitting behind his desk and a person standing up in the courtroom (the foreman of the jury).

Script

1 Guilty!

2 Excuse me?

1 Guilty!

2 Pardon?

1 Sorry . . . guilty, m'Lord.

2 You are the foreman for the jury?

1 Yes, m'Lord and it is an honour and privilege to serve queen and country. *(Smiles at the judge)*

2 I dare say.

1 Guilty, m'Lord. *(Smiles at the judge)*

2 In all my twenty-seven years of sitting on the bench this is, I can categorically state, the quickest verdict ever reached.

1   Thank you, m'Lord.

2   In fact, this will make courtroom history.

1   Really, m'Lord?

2   Definitely, it's never happened in court before.

1   No, m'Lord?

2   No, not in the history of justice has a court decided a man's guilt before the trial has started!

1   He is guilty, m'Lord.

2   Without hearing any of the evidence, listening to any of the witnesses, what, may I ask, has led you to this inspirational verdict?

1   He looks guilty.

2   He looks guilty?

1   Yes, m'Lord; eyes too close together, definitely a shifty character, looks like a thief.

2   The man in question is on trial for vandalism.

1   Oh, I see, um, oh . . . (Coughs a couple of times) . . . didn't he pinch something before his spot of vandalism? A quick smash-and-grab, kind of thing?

2   He did not steal a solitary item, not a brass farthing.

1   He does look like a thief, m'Lord. You've got to admit that he does. Look at those eyes. Are they close together or what?

2   Foreman of the jury, Mr Fothersgill is not on trial because of his looks, the colour of his eyes, the closeness of his eyes, the thickness of his eyebrows or the shape of his face. Is that clear and understood?

1   Yes, m'Lord . . . shifty-looking character, though.

2   Would you please stand down.

1   Stand where?

2   Out of the courtroom, to be exact.

1   But why? I'm only doing my duty for queen and country. *(Smiles at the judge)*

2   You are prejudiced, you are biased, you are incapable of listening to all of the facts and making a sound judgement.

1   If I listen to all of the facts, all of the evidence . . .

2   Yes?

1   . . . then can I say 'Guilty'? *(Smiles at the judge)*

2   Foreman of the jury, you are in contempt of the court.

1   Pardon, m'Lord?

2   If you do not leave this courtroom of your own accord, you will be back here before you can say the word 'guilty', sitting where the accused is seated, is that clear?

1   I haven't done anything wrong, why are you getting so upset? I'm a law-abiding citizen; he's the guilty one, your honour.

2   Out!

1   It's in his eyes!

Application

No jury would pronounce judgement without first weighing up the evidence. How about our response to God? Have we sifted through the facts or fallen for false ideas?

Discussion starters

- What evidence is there to believe in God?
- What evidence is there to believe in Jesus?
- What evidence is there to be a Christian?

Bible verses

- Romans 1:18-20
- Acts 17:32-34

Here's one I read earlier!

The message

To introduce the Bible and its message.

Characters

1 = librarian
2 = customer

Setting the scene

A man wandering up and down obviously looking for something. He stops to look carefully then continues with his search. Standing behind a desk piled with books, is the librarian. She is clutching a book in one hand holding it in front of her to read. Aware of the person pacing about she keeps glancing up to take a look.

Script

1   Can I help you, please?

2   I'm looking for a book.

    (Librarian raises her eyebrows.)

1   Really?

2   Yes.

1   Any one in particular?

2   Yes . . . but I'm not sure which one. Can you help me?

1   Um . . . That depends. In our library we have . . . *(Stops to look at some information on desk)* . . . 25,321 books at present. Which one in particular would you like?

2   That's the problem. I'm not sure. I know I want a particular book but I'm not sure which one.

1   Perhaps if you narrowed it down to a category? You know. History, art, science, education, law, biography, fact, fiction, adventure, thriller, romance. Category?

2   I see what you mean. Perhaps . . . *(Librarian leans forward)*

1   Yes.

2   Perhaps . . . history.

1   Ah, history. A favourite of mine. Now which period? Victorian, Elizabethan, Tudor, Dark Ages, World War One, World War Two, twentieth century, medieval?

2   They all sound very interesting but I wanted a book that told me the history of mankind from when we began to how we will finish.

1   *(Librarian looks perplexed)* I don't know if we have such a book.

2   Oh, well, perhaps a book on the law.

1   Ah, yes, we have many fine volumes from the Magna Carta to the concise book of bye-laws on how to treat the countryside. *(Looks very pleased)*

2   Um . . . none of those books. It's a book on the kind of laws which we all have to live by. Moral laws as well as civic ones. How the two are perfectly combined together so we live healthily in our own life as well as with our fellow man.

1   I don't think I have such a book.

2   Oh, well, perhaps adventure.

1   Adventure books, one of my favourites. We have Alistair MacLean, Tom Clancy, John Grisham, Enid Blyton, C. S. Lewis, you name it, we've got it. *(Librarian looks very satisfied)*

2   The kind of adventure I was looking for was one which affected the whole of mankind in the most dramatic and amazing way.

1   I don't think we stock such a book.

2   A book that tells about the fall of man and his redemption, his eternal destiny.

1   I'm very sorry.

2   I could give you the author's name and the title, will that help?

(Librarian brightens up.)

1   Yes, that would be perfect.

2   The author's name is God. The book is the Bible. Do you have one?

(Freeze)

Application

The Bible is a unique book in the whole world of literature as it declares that this book is the word of God. It is the world's best seller because it is a real life-changer, God's living word.

Discussion starters

- What makes the Bible unique?
- How should we read the Bible?
- How does the Bible change us?

Bible verses

- Hebrews 4:12
- 2 Timothy 3:16

Just a piece of paper?

The message

To look at promises.

Characters

1 = customer
2 = shopkeeper

Setting the scene

A shopkeeper standing behind the counter, a customer browsing around the shop. The customer selects a few items and deposits them on the counter.

Script

1   There are some excellent items in this shop.

2   Thank you. I do pride myself on keeping well-stocked shelves of various useful and pleasing purchases.

1   I would like to buy these. *(Places objects on counter)*

2   A good selection. I say, a very good choice. Very practical. Very affordable. Very attainable to the man in the street. If I do say so myself, a very good choice. Wise!

1   Thank you. I'd like to pay for them, please.

2   Of course you would. Of course you would, and what honest citizen wouldn't. I must say you look like a very honest person. Are you honest? Are you?

1   Well, yes, I think so, I try my best.

2   Any criminal convictions?

1   No!

2   Ever told any lies?

1   No!

2   Little white ones, perhaps?

1   No!

2   Just as I thought. A very honest person. Can you turn your head to the side, please?

(Customer turns head)

2   A very honest profile. Unmistakable. Look at that chin, dignified, distinct, definitely honest.

(Customer becoming a little perplexed. Puts a £5 note on the table.)

2   Excuse me, sir, you've dropped a piece of paper.

1   No, that's my money.

2   I beg your pardon.

1   To pay with.

(Shopkeeper picks up the note and gives it a very careful and thorough examination)

2   Looks like a piece of paper to me.

1   It's a five-pound note.

2   Oh yes, I can see it's a note.

1   Good. Now we're getting somewhere.

(Shopkeeper produces a batch of notebooks from under the counter)

2   I've got lots of notes already. Books full of notes. Look. *(Flicks pages of notebooks in the customer's face)*

1   Oh, I can see.

2   I'm glad you do.

1   Very funny. Very amusing. Great sense of humour. Nearly had me going there. Now can I pay?

2   Of course you can. Now what are you going to pay with?

1   My £5 note.

2   Sorry, but I don't accept paper. Got plenty already. Now I could do with a cow. A good milking cow. I like a good pint of milk, I do.

1   A cow?

2   Or a parrot. A talking one, that is. Bit of company in the shop.

1   A parrot?

2   Either one I'd accept.

1   But this is a £5 note. It is legal tender. Look there's the queen's head.

2   Lovely woman.

1   Look at this. The Bank of England.

2   Very swish, I must say.

1   I promise to pay the bearer the sum of £5. I promise, from the Bank of England. I promise! Now will you accept my £5?

(Shopkeeper picks up and studies the £5)

2   Colourful little piece of paper, nice bit of writing on, but no need for paper in the shop.

(Customer picks up £5 and storms to the door)

2   If you come back with a cow . . . or a parrot . . .

(Freeze)

Application

The promise of the Bank of England is good enough for all bank notes whatever their colour or amount. It is a promise that is dependable. Sadly, in life, we find a trail of broken promises. It is great to know that God is faithful to all his promises.

Discussion starters

• Why are promises important?
• Why do we break promises?
• What is God like at keeping promises?

Bible verses

• Psalm 145:13b
• Hebrews 10:23

What a load of rubbish!

The message

To look at what would happen to our lives if we didn't get rid of the rubbish inside of us.

Characters

1 = Mr Swizbank
2 = Mr Wright – man from the council

Setting the scene

Man sitting down reading a paper. He is surrounded by boxes, old papers, sweet wrappers, etc. After a few seconds he stops reading and throws the paper on the floor. At the same time there is a knock at the door. Slowly he walks towards the door.

Script

1   Hello, Mr Swizbank?

2   Yeah.

1   I'm Mr Wright.

2   So?

1   I'm from the council.

2   So?

1   So, I've come to visit you personally.

2   Why?

1   Because you have refused to answer any of our letters.

2   Oh.

1   Did you receive them?

2   Letters from the city council?

1   Yes.

2   Addressed to me?

1   Yes.

2   Dunno.

1   You do not know?

2   That's what I said first time.

(The man from the council peers around him into the house)

1   It looks like you have a few letters in your house.

2   Letters, cards, papers, tissues, sweet wrappers, lots of 'em.

1   And you don't know if you received our five letters?

2   Dunno.

1   Perhaps I should read you the contents of our letter?

2   If you wanna.

(The man from the council clears his throat, peers at the letter in his hand and begins to read)

1   It has been duly noted that as from January 1st *(Use a month that is a couple previous to the one you are in)* there has been no refuse collected from your household. On the various days when our workmen have called at your property we have found no bins to empty, yet we have received fifty-one letters of complaint from your neighbours. One such letter stated the distress caused to an elderly lady who, on putting out her milk bottles on a rather windy day, was hit in her face with something rather pungent smelling. The said item was believed to have come from the vicinity of your back garden. On close inspection by some rather concerned neighbours it was

noticed that piles of rubbish were spreading and multiplying at an alarming rate throughout your garden. One neighbour wrote a rather worrying letter that the price of his house had been drastically reduced due to the strange aroma that now hung over his property. What have you to say, Mr Swizbank?

2   Dunno.

1   You do not know? You do not know? Mr Swizbank it seems patently obvious to me that you have neglected to clear out your rubbish for nearly three months. Your house is a tip, your mess is everywhere and affecting other people's lives too. What are you going to do about it?

2   Dunno.

1   Why on earth haven't you put your rubbish out to be collected?

2   Couldn't be bothered.

1   Do you realise the consequences of allowing rubbish to flourish?

2   No.

1   Ever heard of the bubonic plague?

2   Bubonic plague? No.

1   Disease, Mr Swizbank. Dirt, disease . . . death.

(Mr Swizbank looks at all the mess in the house)

2   Oh rats.

1   Ah, at last you've seen the light.

2   No, I've just seen a big rat run up my stairs, excuse me.

(Turns and freezes. Mr Wright looks alarmed, tucks his trousers into his socks and turns to run. Freezes.)

Application

We know there would be serious consequences if we left rubbish to over-flow in our homes and on our streets. What about in our lives? Not physical rubbish but things which spoil and soil us. Lies. Prejudice, Selfishness. We need to remove the rubbish from our lives. We need Jesus.

Discussion starters

• Why did Mr Swizbank allow the rubbish to build up?
• What should he have done?
• How can we deal with the things which are wrong in our lives?

Bible verses

• Romans 3:23
• Ephesians 4:31-32

Resolutions or revolutions?

The message

To show that we cannot change ourselves no matter how hard we try.
We need the love and grace of God changing us on the inside.

Characters

1 = Val
2 = Sal

Setting the scene

Two women exercising (aerobics). It is hard work but they are both very
determined.

Script

1   Every year the same.

2   Too much to eat.

1   Too much to drink.

2   Too many parties.

1   Too much everything.

2   Every January the same.

1   Time to exercise.

2   Time to lose weight.

1   Time to make a new start.

2   Time to make a resolution.

1+2 This year!

*(Both turn and freeze. When they turn round again the exercise is
definitely taking its toll.)*

1   Every year the same.

2   Lots of good intentions.

1   Lots of aspirations.

2   But in the end . . .

1   It's a load of perspiration.

(Both stop exercising and smell under their arms, making noises to show that it is not very pleasant. They begin to exercise again, slowly.)

2   Why is it so hard to change?

1   Even when you try your best.

2   Year after year it's always the same.

1   By the end of the month we've packed in again.

2   We try and we try,

1   We struggle and strain,

2   And then we give in,

1   Because it's way too much pain.

(Both stop exercising and collapse. Eventually get up and try to get their breath back.)

2   Did you get anything else for Christmas?

1   Apart from all those exercise tapes, diet books and fitness guides?

2   Yeah.

1   No – oh, there was one other thing, but I've not had time to look at it.

2   What's that?

1   I'll show you.

(Val digs into her bag and produces a Bible. Hands it to Sal.)

2   A Bible?

1   Yeah.

2   That's not going to help you do aerobics.

1   I know.

2   Wish I could stick to my resolutions.

1   So do I.

2   Why is it so hard to change?

1   Why can we never do it?

2   Here's your Bible.

1   Don't think I've got time to read that.

(Both look at each other and start exercising again)

1+2 I wish we could change.

(Freeze)

Application

There is a deluge of 'self help' books/videos on the market. Why? Because people want to improve and change themselves. From the way they look to the way they act. What we all need to realise is only a radical change of heart can make a real life difference.

Discussion starters

• What ways do people want to change?
• Why do people want to change?
• How can we really change the way we are?

Bible verses

John 3:1-6
2 Corinthians 5:17

Ship ahoy!

The message

Someone lost out at sea, drifting aimlessly. This is a picture of our lives without God. Along comes a big ship, willing to rescue him. What will happen? What will he do?

Characters

1 = ship's captain
2 = man

Setting the scene

A man standing gazing out to sea, wearing a pair of sunglasses (maybe a cap too), feels the stubble on his chin. Smells under his armpits. It is bad news! Goes to wash himself. He is busy splashing water all over when there is a loud cry in his ear.

Script

1   Ship ahoy!

     (Man stops splashing himself and looks up)

1   Ship ahoy!

2   Oi to you too, shipmate.

1   What are you doing?

     (Man looks at himself)

2   Having a good wash. It's been a few days. Wouldn't get too close if I were you. Hope the wind's not in your direction.

     (Ship's captain has a good sniff. Nearly falls over.)

2   Sorry.

1   Never mind, can't be helped. I don't suppose you've had a nice hot shower, not on your little rickety thing.

2 No.

1 My question, my good man, is what are you doing, apart from the wash and things? I mean, what are you doing out at sea, miles from anywhere, all alone?

(Man looks all around him, looks at himself)

2 Nothing.

1 Nothing?

2 Not really.

1 How long have you been out at sea?

2 A long time . . . *(begins to count with his fingers, muttering to himself)* . . . longer than I can remember really.

1 How have you managed to survive on your own for so long?

(Man thinks about it)

2 Don't know. You just do, I suppose. Night follows day, day follows night. I sleep, live, breathe, play on the raft.

1 Play?

2 Yeah, play, I mean I've got to have something to do.

1 What do you play, out here all on your own?

2 Oh, all sorts – 'I spy'.
(Puts one hand over his eye)
I spy with my little eye something beginning with S.
(Removes hand to be another character)
Sun?
(Puts hand back over)
No.
(Removes hand)
Sea
(Puts hand back over)
Yes.

1   How . . . interesting. *(Little cough)* So where are you going?

2   *(Man looks around)* I don't really know, wherever the current takes me. Sometimes this direction, *(Leans to one side)* sometimes this, *(Leans to the other side)* sometimes I just get blown round in circles. *(Starts spinning round and round)* It can get very confusing.

1   But you don't know where you're going?

2   No.

1   Please let me get this straight. You're out here at sea, on your own, don't know where you're going, don't know how you are going to live from day to day, and that's it?

2   Yeah . . . just about.

1   Just about . . . well, can I make a suggestion?

2   Sure, it's a free world.

1   Why don't you come on board my ship. There's plenty of room. Nice hot showers, lots of fresh water, good food, lots of really nice people here, and we do know where we're going, you could join us. I mean . . . it is a bit dangerous down there, don't you think? You could easily drown and . . . can you survive on your own . . . for ever?

2   That's a good question. Not really thought about that. *(Pauses, suddenly has a thought)* How do I know though that you don't want me on board so you can take my raft?

1   Your raft?

2   Hey, it may not look much but it's all I've got.

1   No, we're not after your raft.

2   How do I know what you're saying is true? Where is your food? I can't see any.

1   If you came on board you would. I suppose you have to trust me, but just think about it. Use your reason. The ship is rather large, isn't it; there's a lot of power here. Don't you think we'll have everything you need here?

2   Um . . . maybe. But this is my raft. All I've ever known.

1   Don't you think there's more to life than bobbing up and down on your little raft?

2   I supp . . . I don't . . . maybe.

1   Look, I'm not going to force you up here. It's your choice. Tell you what, I'll lower a ladder, then if you want to you can climb on up. OK?

2   OK.

1   I'll just go and get the ladder.

     (Man goes towards ship then stops, looks puzzled. Freezes.)

Application

Someone once said that there is a God-shaped hole in every one of us that only God can fill. Without God in our lives there is something vital missing and we are lost and adrift in life.

Discussion starters

• Why is it impossible to survive on our own?
• Why do we need God?
• What sacrifices do we have to make?

Bible verses

• Romans 6:6-23
• John 14:6

Stop or go?

The message

To show the difference of becoming a Christian and being a follower of Jesus.

Characters

1 = walker 1
2 = walker 2

Setting the scene

Two walkers with rucksacks looking ready for a big hike. One of them is studying a map, the other one is simply looking around.

Script

1   This should be a great walk. *(They are looking at the map)* Views from the top of the mountain should be spectacular, especially on a day like today.

2   Yeah, it is a beautiful day.

1   Perfect conditions for walking. Have we got everything we need?

2   Packed it all myself. Plenty of food, your favourite sandwiches, peanut butter, egg and tomato, flask of herbal tea, your Union Jack balaclava, waterproofs, first aid kit, compass, cups, plates and Kendal mint cake.

1   Cuddly toy?

2   Hey!

1   Just joking. Sounds like you have packed everything. I can't wait. *(Folds the map up and puts it back into the rucksack. Takes one big deep breath then sets off.)* Beautiful day, great scenery, a big walk ahead, mountains to climb, perfect, just perfect, what do you think? *(Turns to where he thinks his friend is but he isn't there, looks back*

and sees that his friend is sitting down eating a bar of chocolate!)
Hey, what are you doing?

(2 Holds up the bar of chocolate to show 1 what he is doing)

1   I can see that you're eating but we've only just started. You can't be having a break now, we haven't even gone a mile. Come on, let's get moving.

2   This chocolate is delicious.

1   Sorry, did you hear what I said?

2   About the walk and only just having started and not having time to take a break yet.

1   Yes.

2   Oh, I heard all of that.

1   And?

2   And I've decided,

1   Decided what?

2   To stay here.

1   Here?

2   Well here, actually. *(Points to where he is sitting)*

1   But you can't.

2   Why not?

1   Because we said we were going to go on this walk, together.

2   I know I did, and I'm sorry but I don't think it's a good idea.

1   You did yesterday and this morning, so what's changed?

2   I've been thinking.

1   And?

2   This walk is a long walk, isn't it? I mean it's not just a half-hour stroll. What if I get blisters or twist my ankle and have to walk for miles in excruciating pain? Or what if we get lost on the mountain and the mists come down? What if we meet a ferocious animal waiting to pounce and tear us limb from limb?

1   I think your imagination is working a little bit of overtime here. Look, it is a long walk, there is a mountain to climb, you may even get a blister or two but . . . it will be worth it, the sense of achievement, the exercise, the fresh air, the views, and you did say you would come on the walk. I never forced you to.

2   I know but I am rather comfy here. The views are OK from here.

1   So are you coming or not?

2   I'll think about it.

1   We haven't got all day.

2   I know.

(Both look at each other and freeze)

Application

So many people make a decision to become a Christian but do they continue in their faith? Are we following Jesus today? Jesus said 'follow me'. There is a cost involved. Are we prepared to follow him in our lives today?

Discussion starters

- What do you think about the friend who said he was going to go on the walk but didn't?
- Why did he change his mind?
- Why press on with the walk?

Bible verses

- Luke 14:28-30
- Mark 1:17

The gate

The message

Based on John, chapter 10. Jesus is the only way to God.

Characters

1 = walker 1
2 = walker 2

Setting the scene

Someone standing in a field. He rolls up his sleeves and charges forward, crashing into a wall! Bouncing off the wall, he rubs his face which has just been badly bruised by the rocks.

After a few seconds' thinking time, he tries a new approach. This time he tries to climb over the wall. A few attempts later he collapses on the floor. After a brief rest he stands up and kicks the wall, then hops around on one foot yelling in pain. When the pain subsides he goes to the stile to sit down (step-ladders).

Another walker passes by. She sees the person sitting with his head in his hands. Walking by, she tries to strike up a friendly conversation.

Script

2   Hello. Lovely day. *(Walker 1 gives a grunt)* Going far? *(Walker 1 points forwards)* Oh yes, it's beautiful over there – that's where I'm going. *(Walker 1 grunts)* *(Realising there is not going to be a good conversation or any conversation at all, Walker 2 decides to move on.)*

1   Got a rope?

(Walker 2 stops in her tracks)

2   Pardon?

1   Got a rope? Got a big rucksack – simple question: have you got a rope? I'm not asking you the circumference of the earth or what the square root of 167892 is. Have you got a rope? Yes or no?

2   No.

1   Typical. Well, have you got a pickaxe?

2   Pickaxe?

1   Yeah, you know, the one that you use when you're climbing a mountain. The one with a sharp point. *(Now warming to the subject Walker 1 stands up and demonstrates the pickaxe by swishing his hands through the air. Walker 2 is now looking slightly unsettled, a little worried!)*

2   No, I'm sorry, I don't have a pickaxe.

1   Charming.

2   Sorry.

1   What about a drill?

2   Drill?

1   Yeah, drill. Only, not just an ordinary drill, but one of those big monsters that council workers use. You know which one I mean? *(Walker 1 stands up and graphically acts out someone using a drill)*

2   No, I'm afraid I don't carry one of those around with me. I might have one in my wallet though, shall I check? *(Walker 2 gives a nervous laugh)*

1   Are you trying to be funny?

2   No, no, not at all. I'm just sorry I can't help you.

1   I'll never get there.

2   Get there?

1   That field. *(Walker 1 points forwards. Walker 2 has a look, looks back at Walker 1. Walker 2 looks slightly baffled.)*

2   Why can't you . . . er . . . get in that field?

1   Have you seen the wall?

2   That wall?

1   Of course!

2   Yes, I can see the wall running round the edge of the field.

1   Impossible to climb. Look at this bruise. *(Walker 1 points to his face)* And that one. *(Shows his leg)*

2   I get the picture.

1   What a day. That wall's a real killer.

2   You could try the gate.

(Walker 1 looks, stares, rubs his eyes, looks again. Both freeze)

Application

There is no other way. It is not by works we are saved but by grace, the gift of God.

Discussion starters

• What makes someone a Christian?
• What part does faith have in salvation?
• Why do people try to earn their way/make their own way to heaven?

Bible verses

• John 10:1-21
• Ephesians 2:8-9

The present

The message

To show that sex is a gift from God but must be saved for marriage.

Characters

1 = Albert
2 = Ethel

Setting the scene

A man and wife sitting in their living room enjoying a cup of tea.

Script

1   That's a nice cup of tea, lass.

2   You do like my Yorkshire tea, don't you, luv.

1   *(Gives a good slurp)* Something came in the post this morning.

2   What was that, luv?

1   A present.

2   A present?

1   A Christmas present!

2   But it's not Christmas for months.

1   It's from Uncle Bruce in Australia.

2   Rich Uncle Bruce?

1   Stinkingly rich Uncle Bruce. I wonder what it is? *(Albert goes and brings out the present, rubbing his hands)*

2   We'll find out on December 25th.

1   That's a long time to wait.

2   I know.

      (Ethel has a little peek. Albert feels it. Ethel shakes it.)

1   It's a long, long time to wait.

2   But it will be worth it. The excitement, the suspense, the joy on Christmas morning.

1   The pressure, the frustration.

2   Well, I think we should wait.

1   *(Albert sulks and has a big slurp)* OK. I'll put it away.

2   That's a good idea. If we don't see it we're not tempted.

1   *(Albert grabs it, tears the paper)* Oh, look Ethel, it's open!

2   What!

1   There, I could see what it is.

2   You'll spoil things, Albert.

1   It's nearly open.

2   It's not Christmas.

1   It is our present, for us, who is to say we shouldn't have it now. It belongs to us.

2   It was given to us . . . for Christmas.

1   Merry Christmas – now let's open it. *(Albert looks, beggingly)*

2   Oh, go on then.

      (Albert opens present)

1   All-time greatest Christmas cards. I love Christmas cards. I love Christmas. I love Christmas presents. I love waking up on Christmas morning and opening them all . . . on Christmas Day.

2   We should have waited.

Application

Maybe you've heard the expression 'you'll spoil your dinner' when you are about to nibble on a biscuit shortly before mealtime. There are lots of benefits in waiting for the right moment, i.e. waiting to open a present.

God has given us a precious gift. The gift of sex. The gift is reserved for marriage where it can be enjoyed by people who love one another and are committed to each other for the rest of their lives. Sex outside marriage will only spoil this special gift.

Discussion starters

• Why do we find it difficult to wait for things?
• Why should we wait for marriage?
• What are the potential consequences if we don't?

Bible verses

• Genesis 2:23-24
• 1 Thessalonians 4:3-7

The prodigal daughter

The message

Based on the parable of the prodigal son.

Characters

1 = father/narrator
2 = daughter

Setting the scene

The narrator starts the story. The daughter stands with her back to the audience until her first line.

Script

1   This is the story of a young woman . . .

2   *(The daughter turns around)* I'm a young woman.

1   . . . who was really stubborn and selfish and she always wanted her own way.

2   That sounds like me.

1   Yes. One day she went to her father and said . . .

2   Dad?

1   Yes.

2   I want all my money now.

1   All of it?

2   All of it.

1   That's a lot of money.

2   I know.

1   Because the father loved his daughter he gave her everything she asked for. He gave her . . .

2   Yes?

1   . . . her pocket money.
(Father puts his hand in his pocket, acts out giving money to his daughter)
He gave her her birthday money too.
(Father acts out giving daughter birthday money)
And he even gave her her Christmas money as well.
(Father acts out dragging large heavy sack of money and passes it into his daughter's hands for her to drag away)
The daughter staggered off to spend it all. First she went to the sweet shop and bought lots and lots of sweets to eat.

2   Hmm . . . I want some of those, and some of those, and some of those . . .

1   She ate them and she ate them and she ate so many she felt really sick.

2   *(Makes sound of throwing up)*

1   Arrgh! Next she went to the computer store to buy lots of games to play. She played them and she played them until she couldn't see straight any more. *(Daughter makes appropriate noises)* Then she went to the fairground to go on all the different rides.

2   Wow, Oohh . . . etc.

1   Suddenly she realised she had no more money left. No money meant she couldn't buy anything to eat or drink. She had no more friends. She was really sad and very miserable.

2   I'm really sad and miserable. Nobody wants to be my friend now that I haven't got any money left.

1   Then she remembered her father.

2   Daddy. *(Said hopefully. Pause.)* No, he certainly wouldn't want to see me.

1   Why not? I'm sure your dad still loves you even though you've done all these wrong things. If you went home now I'm sure he'd welcome you back.

2   You don't understand. You see, I've been really stubborn and selfish and greedy.

1   I'm sure he'd want to see you. Please, why not go home and see? Go home to your dad. He would want to see you.

    (Next line said to the audience.)

2   Oh no he wouldn't.

    (The audience are encouraged to join in with the narrator)

1   Oh yes he would.

2   Oh no he wouldn't.

1   Oh yes he would.

2   Oh no he wouldn't.

1   Oh yes he would.

2   O . . . K then.

1   So the daughter set off home wondering if her father would still love her. After all, she had been naughty and selfish and stubborn and greedy. The father stood looking day after day for his daughter's return. One day, in the distance, he could see her walking towards his house. The father ran to the front door, burst it open and charged down the garden path to greet her.

2   Daddy *(Pause)* I've been really stupid, selfish, greedy and stubborn but I'm really sorry now. Will you forgive me?

1   Daughter, I forgive you. Come home now. We'll have a really big party. You can invite all your friends and we'll play your favourite games. Come on.

Application

A daughter and not a son, but the same story Jesus told and the same message too. A story of how we have all gone our own way, turned our backs on our Father God. How we need to come to our senses and turn back to him and when we do – what a response! God loves us to bits and will welcome us with open arms.

Discussion starters

- What was the father's response to the son? What does that teach us about God?
- Where are we right now in our relationship with God?

Bible verses

- Luke 15:11-32
- John 3:3-16

The rescue station?

The message

To look at the responsibility the Church has in sharing the gospel. How sometimes, for various reasons, we fail to do that.

Characters

1 = passer-by
2 = lifeguard

Setting the scene

A woman dashes onto the stage. She is breathless and looks like she has been running for a long time. She reaches a man who is sitting down, relaxing, reading a book.

Script

1   Quick . . . Quick!

(The man sitting down stops reading his book and looks up)

1   You've got to come now, quick!

(She starts to move away, stopping suddenly when she realises no one is following her. Begins to retrace her steps.)

1   Quick, or it may be too late.

2   I'm sorry, I'm not sure if I understand. Are you wanting my help?

1   Of course I am. There's a man drowning out at sea.

2   Oh my!

1   And you are a lifeguard.

(The man sits up straight, puffing out his chest proudly)

2   I most certainly am.

1   So you've got to come now!

2   Drowning, did you say?

1   Yes!

2   Um, that is serious. Now let me look, D . . . D . . . D . . . for drowning. *(He flicks through his book to find the correct page)* Ah, drowning: The intake of water to a rather dangerous level, best remedy is to get out of the water immediately. If you are unable to do this yourself you may need some assistance. Help is essential in order to preserve life. Sounds pretty serious to me.

1   Serious! The man could die! You are a trained lifeguard, aren't you?

(The man stands up indignantly)

2   Trained! Trained, you ask? Of course I am. Look at these. *(He reaches down and picks up a folder. Inside are scores of certificates. Holding them in his hand, he begins to go through them.)* Certificate of Excellence for correct procedure of diving into water, head first, hands together. Certificate of Merit for tying knots. Certificate of Gold Award for pulling boats to shore with bare teeth. Certificate of First Class Honours for collecting all three thousand pieces of litter off the beach. Do I need to go on?

1   You do rescue people, don't you?

2   Well . . . well . . . of course we're trained to rescue people. Why do you think we're here. We don't just exist for the fun of it, you know. I have attended all two hundred and twenty-nine training courses . . . twice. I am the longest serving lifeguard on the beach. I have had this vocation all my life. *(He puts down his folder full of certificates and starts to demonstrate swimming strokes)* I am the strongest, most synchronised swimmer there is. Ask the dolphins, they'll tell you.

1   Have you rescued anyone?

2   I'm . . . what! This is an outrage!

1   Yes or no?

2   I can't believe you're asking such a personal, impertinent question.

1   Yes or no? *(She nods her head and shakes her head to demonstrate)*

2   Maybe I haven't, but that is beside the point.

1   Well now you have your first chance, come on.

2   Drowning, you said?

1   Yes!

    (He sits back and picks up his book)

2   Drowning: The intake of water to a rather dangerous level, best remedy to get out of the water immediately. I wonder if I have a certificate for this?

1   I can't believe this, I'll do it myself. *(She storms off)*

2   You can't rescue someone. You're not qualified. Where are your certificates? How many courses have you been on? Come back! *(Looks down at his book)* D . . . Drowning . . .

Application

A lifeguard not saving lives? Unthinkable. We all know that people in physical danger need help, need rescuing. What about spiritual danger? People need saving. To offer help is our responsibility and privilege.

Discussion starters

• What was the lifeguard's problem?
• Why do people need Jesus?
• Why do we find it hard telling people about him?

Bible verses

Ephesians 2:1
Romans 10:14-15

What have you got to show?

The message

Based on the parable of the talents.

Characters

1 = labourer
2 = owner

Setting the scene

Man sitting on a deck chair. He is wearing a T-shirt, shorts, sunglasses. He has a bottle of suntan lotion in one hand and he is in the middle of applying some when a woman walks onto the stage. The woman stops and stares at the back of the deck chair, the man sitting there is quite oblivious. Slowly the woman moves forward and stands beside the deck chair. The man is suddenly aware of a presence, looks up and jumps up with a start.

Script

1   Hello! I didn't see you standing there.

2   Obviously.

1   Been standing there long?

2   Long enough.

1   Long time, no see, hey? How long has it been? Three years, four?

2   Five.

1   Five years. That long? How time flies when you're having fun. *(Suddenly realises what he has said)*

2   I would have expected to see a difference after all these years.

1   Really?

2　Some difference at least.

1　Could you be a little more specific? *(2 walks around looking in every direction)*

2　I can't see a brick.

1　A brick?

2　Or a stone?

1　Stone?

2　Or cement.

1　Cement?

2　Or any sign of a building at all.

1　Oh, the building! *(Tries to laugh a false laugh which stops abruptly. Clears his throat a few times before speaking.)*

1　The building.

2　Yes, you do remember, don't you?

　　(More throat-clearing and perplexed expressions)

1　Of course I remember. Two floors.

2　Three.

1　Large swimming pool in the front garden.

　　(2 shakes her head)

1　Back garden?

　　(Shakes head again)

1　No swimming pool?

(2 nods her head and pulls out a plan of the house, unfolds it and shows it to the man)

1   That's right – three floors, no swimming pool, I remember now. What plans, hey? Great plans. Terrific house. Brilliant.

2   So where is it?

(1 looks around)

1   It's not here.

2   No.

1   It's not been built. *(These words are mumbled with head down on chest)*

2   Pardon?

1   I'm sorry, really I am. I meant to build it, honest. I even have the plans somewhere. It's just that, well, I didn't want to do it wrong or make any mistakes, didn't want the house to look a mess.

2   So you did nothing?

(Man hangs his head in shame. Freeze.)

Application

Every one of us is a complete original. We are unique. We have different gifts and abilities. We should not bury the talents that God has given us.

Discussion starters

• Why do we sometimes hide our talents?
• How can we discover our gifts?
• How can we and why should we use them?

Bible verses

• Matthew 25:14-30
• 1 Corinthians 12

Whose seed are you?

The Message

Based on the parable of the wheat and the tares.

Characters

1 = deluded person
2 = shop assistant

Setting the scene

Two people working in a shop. One looks very happy and pleased with himself, the other looks quite disgruntled!

Script

1   Have you seen it?

2   What?

1   You know, have you seen it?

2   I'm sorry I don't know what you're talking about.

1   Have you seen . . . the shop?

2   Would that be the one I am working in, the one I come to five days a week, the one I am standing in right now?

1   Yes!

     (He looks very pleased with himself at this great revelation)

2   Yes, I have seen the shop, in answer to your question.

1   But have you seen it?

2   I'm sorry, I'm no good at riddles. Have you seen the shop? Yes, I work here. Have you seen it? Well, that's a tricky one. What is it? Is it the cash till, or is it the ceiling, or is it the floor, could it be you, could it be me, could it be anything I care a jot about? I doubt it!

1   The window display.

2   Pardon?

1   The window display. I think it's my most creative yet.

2   Don't tell me you've touched the display again. Don't tell me you've moved things around in the shop again. Don't tell me you've put your own display up . . . again!

1   OK.

2   OK, what?

1   OK, I won't tell you, but I have.

2   You have. You have! How many times have you done this?

1   Who's counting?

2   39 times and I am.

1   I think this is my best one.

2   Look, I hate to pour cold water on your enthusiasm, I hate to be the one to break this to you . . . how can I say this in a gentle way? YOU DO NOT WORK HERE!

1   Yes, I do.

2   No, you don't.

1   Yes, I do.

2   No, you don't.

1   Do.

2   Don't.

1   Do.

2   Don't.

1   Don't.

2   Do.

1   Ah, you see I do, you said so yourself.

2   Only because you tricked me. The truth is you do not work in this shop.

1   I come in every day.

2   Don't I know it!

1   I always help the customers.

2   You get in their way. They leave very quickly.

1   I put up displays.

2   I put them away.

1   I am always here.

2   But you are not employed.

1   Pardon?

2   You have no contract. You never had an interview. You had the opportunity to apply for the job but you never did. You never met the manager, was never appointed.

1   But I come here every day.

2   The manager didn't take you on. Look, here is my contract. I know I belong here.

1   You don't need a contract, and I have never seen this manager.

2   Well, he owns the shop and everything in it.

1   I do work here.

2   Look, one day the manager is going to come here to his shop. He knows me but he doesn't know you. You may think you work here, you may believe you do, but what do you think the manager is going to say to you?

1   Do you think he will like my display?

(Both freeze.)

Application

Talk from the parable of the wheat and tares. What is a Christian?

Discussion starters

• What makes someone a Christian?
• Who will make a righteous judgement?
• What is our response to God?

Bible verses

• Matthew 13:24-30
• Romans 10:9

Why can't I drive?

The message

To look at how we worry about things in life. How we struggle in our faith, we want control and need to learn to trust God, He is in control.

Characters

1 = passenger
2 = stewardess

Setting the scene

A man is sitting in a seat looking out of the window, there is concern on his face, a look of agitation. He swallows hard trying to keep calm. A stewardess walks by, he catches her arm.

Script

1   How long to go?

2   To go where, sir?

1   You know, the flight.

2   We haven't taken off yet.

1   Oh! Oh no . . . I . . . um know that, I mean I was just checking.

2   Are you all right, sir?

1   Me? Yes. Fine. Topping. Peak of health and fitness. Couldn't be better. *(Stands up, stretches, starts jogging on the spot, stops, takes deep breaths)* Why do you ask?

2   Your face . . . it's gone all blotchy. Only when you boarded the plane you looked perfectly normal. *(Man starts to feel his face)*

1   Are there three red marks on my forehead? *(Stewardess looks and counts)*

2   One . . . two . . . three. They're only little ones. *(Man clutches his forehead and sits down)* Are you all right?

1   Fine. Perfect. If I could have a glass of water, please.

(Stewardess goes off to fetch a glass of water. The man is busy touching his face, wiping the sweat from his brow. Stewardess returns with a glass of water. The man takes the glass and throws the water into his face! Make sure the glass is not very full! Calmly hands the glass back to the stewardess. She takes it and turns to leave. Man looks round, starts to panic)

1   Excuse me, Stewardess, please!

(Slowly she turns. He is nearly standing in his seat, waving. She pauses for a few seconds before going to see him.)

2   How can I help, sir?

1   The pilot.

2   Yes, sir.

1   Do you know if he's done this before?

2   Done what? He doesn't throw water in his face.

(Man looks shocked)

1   No! Not that! I mean has he . . . you know . . .

(Man acts out flying a plane by sticking out his arms and waving them about)

2   Sorry, I'm not good at charades.

1   *(In an agitated voice, rather loudly)* Has he flown before?

2   Yes, he has, sir. I can assure you he has flown on several occasions.

1   Are you sure?

2   I have been on his flight many times myself.

(Man looks slightly reassured)

1   I was just wondering . . .

2   Yes, sir?

1   If I could go into the cockpit?

2   You would like to meet the Captain?

1   I would like to sit in the cockpit.

2   To stay there?

1   Only for the flight!

2   I'm sorry, sir, that's against procedure.

1   What if I was the one flying the plane? Could I sit there then?

2   The Captain is well capable of flying the plane on his own.

1   I can drive a car.

2   I'm sure you can.

1   Couldn't I just put one hand on the wheel?
     (Holds out his hand. Stewardess shakes her head.)
     One finger?
     (Holds out finger. Stewardess shakes her head.)
     I NEED TO BE IN CONTROL!

2   Please don't shout, sir. I think you're a little out of control. Please
     trust the Captain. He is qualified. His is able. He is capable. Why not
     enjoy the flight, relax.

1   You're quite right. *(He smiles at the stewardess. She smiles back,
     turns and leaves. As soon as her back is turned the man stands on
     his chair, acts out trying to leave through the window. He can't open
     it. Starts to kick the glass. Stewardess turns round, sees the man and
     rushes to stop him.)*

2   Sit down, you can't break the glass. SIT DOWN!

(Man turns round)

1   If I can't fly the plane I'm getting off!

2   Please calm down, please trust the captain. You're quite safe.

1   I WANT CONTROL OR I'M OUT OF HERE!

(Stewardess holds out her hand. He looks at her. Freeze.)

Application

Sometimes we struggle in our faith. We feel like we need to be in control of our life and find it difficult to trust God. When we let God have charge of our concerns and cares we will discover that God is in control and he really does know best.

Discussion starters

- Why did the man panic on the plane?
- Why can we trust God?
- What does God promise?

Bible verses

- Proverbs 3:5
- 1 Peter 5:7